Taking the Names Down from the Hill
by Philip Kevin Paul

TAKING THE NAMES DOWN FROM THE HILL

by Philip Kevin Paul

Nightwood Editions
Roberts Creek, BC, 2003

Table of Contents

I

II

III

IV

Published by Nightwood Editions
RR#22 3692 Beach Avenue
Roberts Creek, BC V0N 2W2
www.nightwoodeditions.com

BRITISH
COLUMBIA
ARTS COUNCIL
Supported by the Province of British Columbia

Cover photograph by Tanya Gillman
Interior illustrations by Philip Kevin Paul
Edited and designed by Silas White
Printed and bound in Canada

Canada Council
for the Arts

Nightwood Editions acknowledges the financial support from the Government of Canada through the Canada Council for the Arts, and the Province of British Columbia through the British Columbia Arts Council, for its publishing activities.

National Library of Canada Cataloguing in Publication Data

Paul, Philip Kevin, 1971-

Taking the names down from the hill / Philip Kevin Paul.
Poems.
ISBN 0-88971-182-8

I. Title.
PS8581.A8295T34 2003   C811'.6   C2003-910444-3
PR9199.4.P385T34 2003

TÁN I MÁN, STIWIEŁ TƬE NE S'HELI EꞮ NEȻE

ACKNOWLEDGEMENTS

My brothers—Andy, Remi and Chris—love me unyieldingly and challenge me in the most essential ways. For this I owe much gratitude.

The completion of this book was caused in no small degree by the encouragement and, at times, the sheer insistence of Lorna Crozier, Patrick Lane and Silas White.

My most essential inspirations during the writing of most of these poems were Tanya Gillman, Maxine Thomas-Pape, Bill Jensen, John Elliott Sr., Sandy Cameron, Norrita Hughes and Earl Claxton Sr.

Thanks to David Zieroth and Robert Adams for their encouragement and help early in the editing of this book.

Some of these poems were previously published in *Breathing Fire: Canada's New Poets*, *An Anthology of Canadian Native Literature in English*, *BC Studies* and the *Coast Salish News*.

NEN HÍSW̱KE—Many thanks!

SECTION I

Ceremony

A crow walks
its muddy
kneeless walk
across
a freshly plowed field.

In this light,
I see the crow
as crows are—

so much seems possible.

About the Fire

Now and then I hear his voice
in one of my brothers', calling
from the same basement.

Or, from nowhere, his voice
is suddenly in my mind.

His bitter tones pull me away from whatever I am doing, forcing all reluctance into a knot in my belly. Appearing in the stairway after his third call, even his fourth, that's the way each chore began for me in those days. He is at the back door, one fist wrapped around a coat hook as he steps into his gumboots—always his gumboots, always his red plaid coat and his black toque.

I follow him into our forest, pulling a sweater on as we walk, juggling a newspaper from one hand to the other while I push my arms into the sleeves. All the while, he's well ahead of me walking in quick, necessary strides—his gumboots, his orange chainsaw swinging at the end of his right arm. I imagine at times this is how those fathers must look, the ones who leave for bowling on Sunday nights.

Beginning at our back door, the trail through our forest goes in a circle. Walking behind him, I kick stones while he carefully chooses the day's work site. In the forest, never far from the path, he begins sharpening the saw's every dull tooth. He pauses to point out the best pieces of scrap wood to build a fire, usually limbs blown down in last fall's wind. At times he shows me the broken ends: the appearance of a seasoned piece of wood, its name by smell, its name by taste—its feel.

I begin by closing my hand around a single sheet of newspaper, pulling the corners in from its centre. On four balls of newspaper I lean some dry cedar and against the cedar, round twigs of maple no wider than my thumbs placed side by side. Behind me my father's saw quiets between every block cut from a broken tree and in my mind, always, his glance assesses my work. So often I fail on my first attempt. Sometimes I keep trying until I get it right, other times he stops his saw to show me with the magical fluency of his hands: four balls of newspaper, cedar, maple. . . . Waving the last twig at me like a wand, he explains: *The secret to any fire is to draw its pieces close enough to offer each other heat, but not too close or they will smother the flame.*

At times I think of the fires my father and I sat by: the fires starting as a small flicker peeking from thick smoke; those starting at one end and burning to the other; the ones catching too quickly, burning too far apart; and the perfect fire—a slow burning, long-haired, smokeless fire. If he thinks it is safe, we leave it burning when we are done. Just before we go out of sight, I turn one last time to see it. We leave the circle path by the trail that ends at our back door.

When the Mask Opens

Inside the raven's mouth
an ancient man's face is carved,
capturing the moment he wept
tears potent enough
to put us here forever.

Whatever we call ourselves now.
Whatever we will call ourselves.
It was that ancient man inside the
raven's mouth, driven by loneliness
to despair, who put us here forever.

A man standing at his window
is looking through years
at the dancer flipping open
the raven mask, only in
quick glimpses at first. Then,
at the end of the dance, down
on his knees, the dancer
leaves the mask open,
the raven's mouth agape,
the ancient man's face
forever in anguish.

The man knows that he can't
look through all those years
and remember everything
about being seven and seeing
a dancer perform in accordance
with the mask he wore. Only with
the dull and clumsy prodding of
the adult mind can he recall
the place of dance that rotted
and was burned down, or was
burned down before
it was humiliated by rot
in the times of vast poverty.

Yet when a raven looks at him,
head cocked, from a tree outside
his window, he tries to remember
or to recreate the earnestness in him
from years ago when a similar raven
looked from that very tree and
the boy wanted it to open
its mouth so he could see
what was inside.

Deer Medicine

When you got on the train you went away
from the people who brought you there
and you noticed for the first time the drift
of bodies in the vast day. And you could feel
the stranger in front of you and the one behind
you and beside you becoming frightened,
and what a strange fear leaving is.

The deer looked vaguely in the direction of the
train as it passed the next morning at daybreak
(how you wanted them to please look right in at you).
The train continued working east, but your thoughts
remained peace-stricken, watching the deer's
hot breath rise up like a melancholy daydream.

II.
When you woke on the fourth day of your fast,
what you thought was the strength of your
personal belief was finally what it really was, pride.
And you wept and that last restraint left you,
washed away like human smell will if you stop eating,
never take to fire for warmth and bathe every day.

When a young doe came on that same day, the dew-
laden ferns threw their tears in its path and you wondered:
Is this the deer I've called out from thought?

The bloodmarks and hoof-drag were pointed back
toward the village—what lesson was being offered
if the deer went to the village and died before anyone
who might be there to witness your first kill?

But when you found the deer, she was hardly aware
of you. You were lonely, sick from hunger and full of
a terrible peace as it chewed the leaves from a salal bush
and spit into the wound you had made in it.

When you had finished thinking out the meaning
of your first kill, maybe a month later, real peace
finally came and it was nothing like sadness.
You lay down where the deer had lain dying,
and it began to rain into your opened eyes.

A Pheasant on Deer Mountain

It is early in spring and morning,
before the sun has arrived.
There is just enough light
to mark the path—a shadow,
darker than twisted trees
guiding it into the morning. She is
little more than a silhouette
when she steps one step then
another from behind an arbutus tree
into the wet path.

There is just enough light
that she can see
I am a man and not a bird.

Because she has no words
and I have no song, she accepts
and I settle for a safe distance between us.

She was designed to disappear.
If she hid,
I would pretend not to see her.

She stays on the path ahead of me
and we stop three times
before we reach the top of the hill:

we stop in a clearing
and have a look at each other;

I wait while she has a drink from the creek;

we stop once to listen.

I have come as far as I am able
when we reach the top of the hill.
I hear her leave.

The sound of her disappearance,
the sound of her soft body
beating into the morning air.

The sound of a stone
and the stone's echo
rolling down the stone slope:

the idea of me standing on the edge
of the small valley
while she lands in the meadow below.

Water Drinker

The music in trees
is water. The only way

of learning that still counts:
I learned this summer
how a tree is a reflection
of a river or a stream.

A tree is like ancient love:
the love my parents gave me
came from a long ways away,
was divided over and over. *The oldest river*
will have the most branches.
It is the only thing
that remains uncomplicated,
grows outward and remains
uncomplicated.

How do you know these things?

The man, sick of the story and of his life, says:
I spent twelve years with the same river
measuring everything to learn
measuring is irrelevant.

There is only time
and looking.

After twelve years you can finally imagine
how a river grows old
and how the trees around it   grow old.

They grow outward and remain uncomplicated.

I sat by a fishless stream for days
this summer, the place I fished
when I was as small
as I remember being.
I felt in the heat the hope in me
being washed over and diluted.
I felt this way without knowing
the fish had all disappeared—

I'd imagined them all summer
swaying lazily in the dark,
murky water at the bottom of the stream
and the flash of their white bellies
as they twisted into the terrible light,
fighting at one end
of a handline.

Here—I bring you to the place
of maples, where on this steep hill
there is only one arbutus, the way
the blood from a fish looks
resting in the stones.

You can feel the stream
on that hill like a small animal
shaking in your hands. Its rhythm
comes up through the ground
just where the water is
about to roll over the edge.

Imagine what the Old People thought
when they saw one small red tree
growing between the grey-
white bodies of the maples.
Imagine their thoughts
when they realized
every stream has its own song
from the shape made by the trees around it,
the sound of the water
turning in the hollow,
returning to them from the leaves.

How long did they sit here
on this perfect flat rock beside
this single arbutus
to finally see
the trees around it were dying
because they weren't as deeply rooted?

When I tell you the word
is still old, I say that
because the first time
a man said ḰO, ḰO, ᵼLĆ,
said *water drinker*,
it was because the generations
before him had sat on the rock
and looked at the tree.
They sat in name of the tree,
as in a song too familiar
to hear, and finally
recognized it. And when
I say the word now, ḰO, ḰO, ᵼLĆ,
it is the same word,
but said in an alien light.

Last Night

Miles away from any city,
a real darkness holds the men close
to the light of the fire. A raccoon,
really the ghost of a raccoon, lifts its nose
and pokes at the smoky air, unbothered
by the men slipping in and out of
the ragged hutch of light. It has waited
before in human air and knows
where the light stops is a darkness
human eyes can't use.

The history of raccoons,
a change that may have unfurled in them
as slowly as a tree's coming of age: just one
raccoon waiting in a parallel darkness
on the edge of the mining camp
that became the village that became
the city; the raccoons that followed would,
without the ability to reason, disappear
into the low horizon of smoke toward
the soft glowing heart of a dying campfire—
the return to that heart unmistakably
the leaving behind of another.

Humans haven't always been
like this either, moved once by the fire
going out in the rain and no other way
to keep warm; a hole in the tent
and no way to fix it; making it through
the winter with every finger and toe,
the potatoes just lasting to the first crop.
All of this before their own time-
swayed shift: real fires no longer
needed, real tents not really
needed, the real winter
no longer real.

The raccoon has waited here
on the last night of many hiking trips,
where many have stooped down to taste
with an alien tenderness this place
in the blood's memory, the mind's
astonishment. These men have been here
at the mouth of this stream before, their
favourite place for a last camp-cooked meal.
The raccoon is anticipating, as are the men,
the dying of the fire. The raccoon,
always beyond reason, will slip into the camp.
The men, lying in their tents,
will be closing down the distance
between their minds and the light
of the city.

ĆÍAAĆU

The way night goes west, followed by
deer, the carriers of dawn.

They shy-step
behind their leader into the meadow
from the bush-stifled hills, as though
from someone's private thought
into plain sight, as though to console
the crying of the Old People in me:
a century of wailing finally coming to tears.

No Hunting in the Place of Deer.

The deer lower their heads into the mist
one by one
and then all at once—raise them.

With a snort and two sharp stomps
their leader hurries them through
the meadow, back into dark woods
and down their great-grandfather's path
toward spring ocean, spring tide.

Maybe everything has gone as planned,
by *some* plan, but I still want to know
why no one said a word when someone
fenced off the Place of Deer, and what
the Old People ate when the spring came
and they weren't allowed to hunt.

Just one word.

ĆIÁÁĆU, name of the spring hunt.

ĆIÁÁĆU, name of the sick deer and
the tide that leaves salt to cure them.

ĆIÁÁĆU, the one word waiting
behind a salal blind to erupt
from its own eternity of silence
and run down the hill.

The Last Forever

A man with cells like yours was half-asleep
in midday and had been fasting. In the half-
awareness of suffering he cast a startled glance
toward the bird, a blue jay, and it seemed
the first beautiful thing.

By then the intentions of things and times
had been all but forgotten, so the man
worked purposefully in the pine hills
to bring down with him a precise name
for this new and difficult era. Yet the bird's
appearance was the first flicker
in the living world to be called coincidence
by the man and it would remain in the family.

The blue jay splashed into the well of light
made by the trees and sun working together.
It was frightened, after touching
down lightly, by the man's careless glance
and when it went back up through
that one tunnel of light, squawked miserably
and shit on the spot—and there
the red seed was.

The man crawled over and buried the seed.
Or the man returned to the spot disheartened,
after failing to go back into the old world,
and happened upon the seed. After that,
he carefully tended to it. Or he came back
years later and believed the small red tree
was from the seed he had buried.

Whatever the case, there it is:
the great, great grandchild of that original tree,
dying now, and we return here with the dull
song in our bones to tend to
some other part of ourselves.

Living in Circles

Alila said if she were a bird, she'd probably get lost. We spent half the morning climbing the hunched mountain next to the village, then we tried to name landmarks we thought we recognized or were close to what we thought should be there. We could not see my house nor the house she grew up in, but I pointed just south of us to what seemed to be our grandmother's place. *It's crazy*, she told me, *I have no sense of direction.* I can sense this fear in me at times, though usually when I'm trying to understand what makes us so different from one another. It will be dark soon, and I wonder how I will find my way home.

Already the darkness is forming a smaller circle around me: some trees not-so-distant shadows, the trees in front of them grey bodies without detail, and close around me the trees defined by a deep orange flame—the small fire I have built. The maple canopy is no more than the light it has allowed to escape, the leaves shifting in the slight breeze, the sky behind a grey flicker. A slow-flying bird beats the air and its vague shape appears and disappears in the gaps between the leaves. When it is gone, I am left with a plain silence.

I try to imagine what the bird saw as it flew by. Maybe just a tiny orange flash and the pale, diminishing circles that follow, me near the centre—a strange being dreaming into the trees. Maybe the bird saw Alila wandering toward her mother's home by the ocean, and our grandmother in her window looking out into the road, and on the edge of my final circle, strangers, like dark birds drifting by.

SECTION II

A Fish on Pandora Street

The Indian man leans in the archway.
The red door behind him opens
to his pocket of night,
to the odd mood of night
kept there in mid-afternoon.

The slow blues is released
from the tavern,
then the night is closed-in and the music
gone.

The man with his rounded mouth
is smoking. His sad daydreams
are with him as he sucks absently at the cigarette,
and blows the smoke into the walkway,
brown tobacco evaporated

into white smoke. His true form
eludes us until he walks away
and the smoke from his cigarette
swirls in an eddy of air around him.

It is as though someone could jerk him
out of that air
and he would not know
what went wrong.

The Violet Light of Healing
for Cecil Malloway

I saw a violet light
      rising,
then arch with its aching back
like a grandfather might
to kiss his grandchild's
worried brow.

What is that light?

And since the question didn't
surprise you,
      you answered:
It's the light that stays
around until
the healing is done.

Remembering the first time
you saw such a light
you recalled also
what it meant to you:
our old country was still
alive somewhere.

You were digging for
camas bulbs in mid-winter
you were so hungry.
When you opened
a certain piece of earth,
violet light
poured out. You were young
and your young self thought
it meant the ground there
was fertile so you kept digging
with your bleeding hands
into the frozen ground.
But you went to bed hungry
that night. Even in your closed eyes,
sleepless, the light wouldn't cease
and through the hole you'd made
in the ground you saw
the violet fields of camas
from happier days of poverty,
when you truly thought
you were poor because
your mother and father
had no money.

So it was that your mother
picked nettles for soup,
even the ones hard and too old,
and your father, with
a hatchet-roughed stick,
dug for camas bulbs,
soft and too young.

Toward the Beautiful Way

It wasn't after she was turned
into the blue jay. And not
at the moment she found
an inherent beauty in all things.

It was the morning she awoke,
tired of the reluctance eating
at her insides like ants,
and the dumb blindness
of daily routine
bringing her to the shore for seaweed,
then back to camp again.

Not the grace in the hand going up
into the sun-crowned air
and coming back down with
the wet, shining fruit—just
the chain-labour of days
and the ants eating at her insides.

On that morning when she awoke
to the unsolved world in her
and around her, she found
the questions
finally not worth asking—
a doubt more like forgetting.

She noticed her own people,
good people, were tracing with
the same dumb blindness
footpaths worn simply
by being walked upon
over and over.

It was understanding, as in
dreams we suffer through,
that you need first to realize
that there is a way out,
then getting through
will only take time.

Mother's Day, Running for Daffodils

Julian runs like a man,
although he is only eleven
years old. His chest is out and
his head is up, a sole purpose
of going forward. The daffodil glow
shines up under his chin, and I
realize for the first time that he
never seems glad at all, even in
the hours such as these
after school on a Friday.
The humiliation of mathematics
and social studies disintegrates
behind him like smoke as he runs.

Russell runs the way I imagine
Santa Claus would run. He's fat,
at least in the way young boys are fat:
all skinny 'cept for his round belly.
Like Julian he is eleven
and the magic's got him good.
His skin's much too dark to show
the glow of the fields, but the magic
is with him—I can tell by how high
he lifts his knees as he runs.

Vinny runs like a pheasant,
in quick, jerky strides with his head up,
feathered hair flicking back like a tail.
The afternoon hasn't changed *him*
although he's crossing the same field
as the others. Maybe it's because, like me,
he turned twelve almost half a year ago
and is bewildered by these absurd days.
The light reflected by the field
catches on the white underbelly
of Vinny's cap, sharpening
the edges of his dark eyes.
It is a darkness I dare not
concern myself with too much.

It's like when we crawled
under the fence at the edge of the field
after deciding only the flowers
in the distance were worthwhile.
Once we started running,
there was simply no turning back.

Only By a Greater Sense of Forgetting
for Little Bird

In the mountains, the place
I always go when I am afraid.
In my country, Saanich,
you in Borneo three oceans away—
an earthquake and tidal wave that followed
wiping away five villages.

From my mountain peak, no way
to reach you in that jungle—
your voice still echoing in my head
through cracks in the phone line.
That one last thing before you hung up:
I don't want to go without
saying how much I love you.
As big as the sky anywhere.

Your postcard taking seventeen days to arrive. Sent
seventeen days before the disaster. On the front,
white sand beaches and—damn—blue water, all seen
from way up. On the back, a small ache of words:
I spent the whole day climbing a strange round mountain,
and when I looked down, this is what I saw.
Kevin, I just had to dance.

On my way home through the sharp rock hills of Saanich
and the fir-tree darkness—the absence of which also makes
Borneo strange to you. There is that one place, remember?
A clearing on a steep hill that leans the weight of an entire
world against the mind. And there's our green ocean
and our blue sky, and all other things that were
once nameless and not strange and not between us.

A Summer Snowfall

Toronto invaded by swarms of aphids
-Toronto Star headline August 3, 2001

Aphis glycines: only the tourist
would look it up with unabashed urgency.
It's a summer snowfall I suppose,
but a distant second in conversation
to the plague of this summer's heat.

A lady in a black dress
on her lunch break sits at a café
alone and brushes them lazy-handed
from her eyes and off the shoulders
of the thin, knitted sweater she has on
over her black dress.

A man on a bike, waiting for the light
to change, teeters back on his seat
and jabs at the air trying to catch some.
He checks his palms between attempts
and in his glance I see remnants of
less busy days and the adventurous curiosity
of new things. When the light changes,
he wipes his hands on his shorts
and steps into his pedals
as I've seen riders
encourage their horses
into a gallop.

A man sweating unashamedly through his grey
T-shirt looks into his coffee and smiles the way
one smiles at common amusements
in an uncommon context.
He even stirs at them, just a bit,
with his index finger,
then goes on looking out at
the people drifting by in the haze of heat.

Not any of it is the way it would be at home.
We'd be appalled and certain
it has never happened before.
We would be sure it was a sign
of more terrifying things to come.

Through the Broken Doorway
for Matthew (1973-1998)

The dog's out front looking
punished and humiliated.
The front door is broken, busted
in spots as though hit with
a sledgehammer. It's hanging
from the one hinge still holding.
The dog doesn't know me
well enough to come, so she goes
out toward the marsh at the other
end of the yard where a brittle rope
hangs lifelessly from a rotting tree—
it's the rope we swung on as children,
went out over the marsh to feel that
unnamed ache above the stomach
and below the heart.

The windows of the house are curtained
and dark. And there is no noise except
the occasional car coming and going
forever down the long, narrow road,
and the dog's high-pitched whines
as she shivers.

On the other side of the doorway,
clumps of mud, as though fallen
from cleated boots, ascend the stairs
and disappear into the dark insides
of the house.

When I go through the doorway,
I get down on my hands and knees,
thinking it somehow wrong to touch
the broken door. A familiar but unnamed
vulnerability grows as I crawl into the
angular light made by the hanging
door, the house's darkness and the cruel
brightness of the day.

As my eyes and heart adjust to the dark,
a muttering—imagined or otherwise—
rises then fades suddenly as when
a moth flutters against your ear.
Up the stairs, the mud tracks
are headed toward Matthew's room
and light in the hallway wavers
because it is from a lamp or a candle.

Finally I am able to make out
Matthew's voice   praying
in our own tongue, a language he didn't
have enough time to finish learning.

Despite everything I know about
this place, this dark, his voice
moving away while I attempt to draw near,
I go insistently on.

From Grandma to Sina

When it was common
for people to be
magic, they knew what
passing through the earth
really was, but they failed
to foresee how different
it would be for us,
the unenchanted.

Look, she's growing old
and is not at all concerned.
She is from those fortunate days
and looks oddly at our sadness
for her, for ourselves.

What she learned from them
she can't explain, so
no longer tries.

She saw *them* try—when
there were still more of them
than there were of us. How they
pounded their fists on the tables
where we sat for dinner!

And for those born within the girth
of uncertainties, I am doing my part.
I have turned out the otherwise-empty
pockets of night that I might find
for you, Sina, the youngest
of my family, what came from then
and too soon will be wholly yours.

Silver Lake, July

If you were here,
would the light busting
through the trees fall
with a better mastery

of grace? You and I

were walking, years ago
now, and along the path
to the Place of Deep Eyes
you stopped and exclaimed,
Oh, this is good light here!
Later you stopped to explain
what happens in a photograph
with bad light, as in the place
we had come to, where the moss
and seaweed-covered rocks
darkened our faces.

If you were here, would the
wind's apathetic roll across
the lake mean less and hurt less
in my night's recollection of

the day? Would we remember,
after working it together,
the song you were singing
when you sang faultlessly
and without restraint
because you didn't know

I was listening? Lover,
teaching me the true nature
of a mile, of all these miles.
Even if I was home,
the distance between us
has grown opaque,
sparsely lighted.

Here, we would be able,
because the lake is warm
enough to swim in and the air
warm enough for dreams,
to grasp what is offered us:

a forgetting
during the bright hours
that the nights keep coming
on and on and the days
grow shorter as the
summer grows dim.

Gabriel Bartleman
(1913-1999)

Saanich is really here
and really here even now.
At my cousin's place in Vancouver,

I am at home. I feel compelled to call her
"auntie" because in a time not so long ago
I would be encouraged to do so—a time we
clumsily call the old days, as though its ways
were no longer with us.

We had gathered in Vancouver to
pray with a cherished friend. We still do
that well and properly: gather for each
other when a gathering is needed.

It was the morning after those prayers
and my uncle went to the telephone
to receive a call from *home* and by then
we knew that such phone calls
could close an era, and that phone call
did just that. Uncle Gabe had died.

My auntie sighed, turned her face down
and began to weep. Her brother stood
behind her and put a hand on her shoulder,
the withholding of his own tears apparent
by the rigid way he stood there and the deliberate

tenderness of trying to comfort his sister.
The room was darkened by a cloud
covering the sun, maybe by the thoughts
that made me feel alone.
Since that day I've often pondered

the varied episodes of Uncle Gabe's long life.
He hit a man over the head with a shovel once,
on a work site he was in charge of,
back when "Indians" weren't often in
such positions, back when a man
could get hit over the head with a shovel
and be deemed, by any witnesses,
to have had it coming and that was that.

I also recall how his joking moods
put us all at ease at family gatherings
and how, through stillness, he could make
us listen. All my life it had been this way:
when he spoke, we were aware he might not
offer such a view again—that he might not
have the time to.

Saanich really *is* here
and really here even now.
At these pages

where I've come to seek perspective
on someone who was old all my life,
small and round without ever seeming so.

Happy, the youngest of my three brothers says,
when I ask him what comes to mind upon
hearing Uncle Gabe's name. This surprises me
since they spent much time at odds. On the other
hand it occurs to me for the first time that Uncle,
like any other man, might be recalled
as a happy man, satisfied and at ease with
the story of his life.

Stories, says the second-eldest brother.
And it's true: he delivered himself through
stories. Ones that were like thinking out loud,
ones deliberate and aimed at the occasion,
stories to wake us when he saw our lives slowing,
stories marking what had changed
and what had not.

Passionate, my oldest brother says
and I recall that too often
his passion was mistaken for recklessness—
mere anger.

Ćáá, says my uncle—the one who received
the phone call—meaning *work* and offers
an explanation: Uncle loved to work.
I remember, then, Uncle Gabe saying to me
on a work site, *Pretending to work,*
no matter how convincing, still doesn't get
as much work done as real, hard work.
Meaning I wasn't fooling him and I wasn't
working hard enough.

After Mom died, he often came to my place
worried that I was living alone now.
He once threw water on me in my bed,
proclaiming it was a serious matter, getting
out of bed in the morning, especially
at times like these! Over coffee, before

sunrise, I heard for the fourth day
in a row the story about the graveyard
where my parents are buried. It had been
relocated there even before Uncle Gabe's time,
a time when there was nothing uncertain
about work needed to be done and *how*
it was to be done. Of this occasion he was fond
of saying: *If horses had toes, these horses pulling the sled*
danced up on there toes, on the spot, before going ahead.

With each telling of the story he devised
a new emphasis, but each time I was to take
special note of two things in particular:
that my Auntie Josie was there on that day and
it was through her that the story had travelled,
and that the relocation was the effort of many
families working together. Showing the

concern I had long associated with him,
he explained:

It is this kind of work
done in this way that I fear
you will never witness in your time.

Patient

I heal my mother
by sitting in this room
with her.

I heal her
in the prayer
of three slow cups of tea.

In the hospital
for two months,
she wants just
small details
about our house.

We close our eyes
and see each room
one by one.

SECTION III

Still Falling

Below the burial ground, KENNES
has taken to its winter form, the echo
of its rhythm stumbling
into this ceremony of grief.

> KENNES is the name of the stream
> and the name of the whale
> that died in the mouth.
> I say the word and I can see the whale
> that beached itself there
> and the ancient man who found it,
> the fresh water of the stream
> falling around this enormous, slow-breathing creature,
> the whale feeling its own weight
> for the first time.
> I am standing with the man just briefly
> as he says, 'KENNES,' and looks into the waterfall,
> then at the whale
> washed up on the shore at low tide.

The winter has always been hard on us.

But when a family stands here together,
we know just what family is:
look how we hold on
to each other as we see
the casket sink into the ground,
my uncle's body

inside. Each of us holds a corner of this story,
though some of us have no hands
to speak of.

It's true,
when I feel helpless
I am the only one
who feels this grief.

       KENNES is the name
       of the stream and name of the whale
       that died in the mouth. I say
       the word and I can see
       the whale that beached itself there
       and the ancient man who found it,
       the fresh water of the stream
       falling around this enormous, slow-
       breathing creature, the whale feeling
       its own weight
       for the first time.

How long had whales returned here
before this one? How long had people
come to witness their return?
To see them chase the young salmon
into the small bay,
nearly to the foot of the falls.

The body of a whale is like any body:
the canoe for an ancient spirit. The water,
like time, moving to the same edge on and on. . .

Still,
I feel as though I am witnessing
the first whale to wash ashore here.
My father's last living brother.

Uncle,
our last handshake in Saanich,
this shovel full of dark earth
on your grave.

Silver Lake, December

The sleeping body of the lake—
I lie my gaze across
its untouched skin
and find hidden pathways
in the story that led us here.

Of the trees surrounding,
I believe not one of them has
its back to us. They sway with then
against the wind's new apparel,
the snow, on this day—the year's
darkest and shortest.

Even our own tracks,
not a full hour old,
are gone now.

The snow brushed lightly
over us as we walked, pulled
from our tangled thoughts
the ones

that don't belong,
yet left behind the question
of a complete healing—

the few brown leaves
still hanging on; the trees
with their ancient limbs
held over us, palms down;
the wind dressed for
this season; the lake's
ambiguous offering.
All of these in the cabin
now turning with me,
falling with me
asleep.

The Emerald Ring

I'm leaving, she says, and I watch after her
even before she leaves, because in such a broken
day anyone can see the future. Because in the future
we do as we did in the past. The line between the two
is an infinitely fine ring we pass through,
unknowingly, yet with a remote and distant
wail against all change, against all things
we are learning in bareness for the first time again.

When she turns to leave, she goes in
her melancholy way down the path,
asking me not to follow. I think of the ring
I'd always meant to have made for her,
engraved with two ceremonial beings
travelling in opposite directions
but bound by inevitability
to meet at the ring's
underbelly. There a fire is carved,
or something with the same *weight* as fire
but does not invoke the harm in things
that rise and fall before becoming
ashes and dust.

And at the crest of the ring
there is an emerald like a shining willow leaf
she held once in her trembling hand,
which somehow evokes for me the song
the bells outside my bedroom window give
when the wind comes to sweep away
the night's fragile things.

My Own
for Philip Christopher Paul (1933-1992)

Imagining your indestructible drop. A tear?
Even between lives I imagine it is with you, your
motherless life. Tuberculosis, when you were eight.
Cancer—your father before you were ready.
Cancer—your own beliefs driving you from
calm when you said you were dying
before you were done. Our hearts as bare as fire
at the brittle August fields when you told me so.

The indestructible drop endures, of course,
but is laden with salt that will not dissolve.

What did it mean to live through such
brutal times and to carry them with you, inside you?
That you felt unsatisfied and too young at the altar
of inextinguishable tasks that you could not let rest?

When I imagine your indestructible drop
encumbered with salt and what will
travel through with you
into the other forms of your life,
I can finally grasp how separate our deaths are—
and that *your* death is not tragic.

The Bare Story of My Life

I was born in a time when the heart wasn't well
understood. My mother was alone with me
in the hospital most of each day,
though whenever he could, my father came
to be with his dying son—after work,
through visiting hours
and more. He would lift me, as though
practicing something new and ceremonial,
away from the machines I was connected to
with wires the colour of blood. In his story
of this time, he mentions it twice—
they were the colour of blood.

And the circular pads stuck to me
to monitor the patterns of my deformed heart,
they were a sickly grey, *cold and hopeless.*
My mother and father took turns cradling me
alone at the quiet end of the hospital.
How odd to think of it now—that in
their stories about this time they are
never together with me in that room.

A few days before I was released
from the hospital, and after it had been
determined I wasn't going to live long,
a stranger arrived in the doorway
of the quiet room. My father would
often recall beholding a man
whose *simplicity lives with him
like a great gift.*

"I wish for this child a great life"—
the stranger's words called a tear to his eye,
which he captured with his index finger
and placed with no small sense of grace
at my right temple. Then he turned to leave,
barely acknowledging my father sitting there,
holding me with an awkward beauty.

When I think of my life before conception,
how difficult my decision to come here
must have been, knowing the pain I would
cause my mother and father in those early
months. Knowing how much later when
my brothers and I were left alone here
together, I would trouble them by being lodged
so deeply in my own story. My mother

never forgot, despite the going on of my life,
that I was her ill child. And my father
eventually told me that in the days after my birth
he must have appeared to be celebrating—but
he was lifting his glass as though at a wake,
in tribute and praise to his dying son.

Francine's Snow

A heavy snowfall comes to Saanich,
a wet snow falling like fat ash into
the field where my cousin Francine
and I built a snowman whose head
was too big for the two of us
to lift into place.

Saanich is not a winter place
for children. By eight years of age
we already had a practiced sense of panic
when the snow came, to get out there
before it melted, turned to slush
with wet blotches of grass
showing through, looking like
shadows under the trees.

                *

I remember the bus rides
to your place. Can you hear
the song of the gears, the sigh
of the doors opening? The discomfort
of being alone and that small,
of walking out past all those people—
and being that small.
In the street, I would
kick at the dirty snow
until you arrived to meet me.

*

All this started
with the smell that belongs
only to the year's first snow.

Then the urge to call you arose.
Then that strange coldness
came in through the closed window
and into my house. It's the coldness
that belongs only to that walk
in the forest when we held onto each other
as deeply and as far back as childhood,
behind the light of a kerosene lamp,
behind the blunt silhouettes
tangled in the hooked shadows of trees—

blanketed people with their fists
pushed up around their necks, though
the snow and cold was impossible
to keep out. And that sharp wavering
of fire we gathered around, built
of Father's precious belongings, offered
a warmth less wanted than the cold—
the ash falling flake by flake around us.

When the Night's Geese Finally Arrive

I recall love lived
in the world as it was in
my daydreams of love—
because I hadn't loved yet.

It was the plastic pail
a child carries searching
for a snake or a frog or,
with any luck, a small dragon
broken lose from father's silence,
raging delightfully in the pail.

And if anyone asks me,
I tell them holding
a hummingbird in your hand
is exactly as they might
imagine, though I could only
be disappointed when I held
the one fallen
freshly from the cat's mouth
and halfway to death,
its life more impossible
because it was dying,
its eyes deepening
as its breath slowed,
a death made more impossible
by my disappointment.

Whoever said it first
—*Geese sing a sorrowful song*—
I believe you now.

However lost I feel
in the world's plan for me,
they have planned *their* arrival.
They know I am for the first
time feeling truly alone,
praying *love, love, love*
to ghosts of real sorrow.

Winter Birds
for Frances Paul (1941-1997)

Chased up close to the house by the snow and cold,
the winter birds are quivering, small and weak,
and falling asleep on their feet, here at the end
of my mother's life. Her late father called them

angels because there is no such word in our language,
and from the story of their creation he saw them
as examples of the potency of innocence. The concept
of angels seemed a fantastic mistake to him, implying

that wisdom and compassion are kind and gentle.
My mother, noticing more and more birds huddling
near the back door in the half-moon shape of melted snow
made by heat escaping the house, wonders aloud why

her late husband, while calling them *rugged survivalists*
to encourage us not to interfere, once backed his Chevy
into the great towering trees in our yard to relieve them
of the burden of a similar snow that was collapsing roofs

and snapping power lines all over the city. She loved
my father for such inconsistencies. He hated our cat,
for instance, yet couldn't bear its growing old, so
warmed milk for it and gave it its own place in the house

for its final years. My mother is again considering
these two voices—of her husband and father—
out loud with me, as though somewhere in their
thoughts is the key to her own struggle.

On our side of what has become "the bird's door,"
she has hung a sign reading *Do not disturb*, which means
to me: *Wait.* She was making the decision while gently
tending the fire and stirring the milk in my tea

into a foggy bloom. If she feeds these winter birds,
they will likely return next winter looking for her.
Over tea and toast at lunch she breaks bread
into pieces she imagines small enough

for their beaks. They are so weak they don't even
flinch when she scatters the first handfuls for them.
How does my mother interpret the incident?
She says, stopped in the hallway with laundry

she barely has the strength left to carry:
I believe I've been a good person. I don't believe
I deserve to die so young. Especially since I've
tried and tried and I can't find the way

to accept it.

Belly Button

My mother was careful
about what she ate
when it was my turn

inside her. It was already me
well before she had problems
getting up out of chairs.
Already me before I had elbows
to poke her with,
her hand on her tight skin
waiting for my next move.

It was my presence in her,
my nearly unstoppable growing,
that made her breasts tender,
her tailbone sore,
made her hungry
and ill. So many times

she has spelled out the odds
I was up against:
her joke about my arrival,
the pill in my tiny fist.

When I was old enough to be
curious, I asked her
about the small round hole in my tummy.

She said, *That's your belly button;*
it used to be your mouth.

SECTION IV

The Cost

a song

Outside night and morning are shaking hands.
Night says *Good morning*, morning says, *Good night*
and under the oak tree where my father used to stand
the snow is rotting. It's just a matter of time.

I hope of all the things that remain,
we don't dwell too long on what we've lost
and when we truly know what has been gained,
love outweighs the cost.

Outside the wind is scratching her back
on the leafless trees whose ancient hands are strong.
The wind sings praise for the things that pass,
and I swear she's singing my mother's song.

I hope of all the things that we've gained,
we don't pine too long for what we've lost
and when we look back up to see what remains,
we see love outweighs the cost.

So the leaves get dropped and then they're kicked around,
by Wednesday they'll be ash.
Funny how the rain turns all our faces down,
till all the world seems at mass.

I hope of all the things gone strange,
we don't believe we will always be lost,
please let me hold you completely for a change
and let our love outweigh the cost.

If This Is the World

A pine tree, its hands raised,
the cloud behind it gone

grey. How the light is softened
by the soft grey hair of the cloud,

how the wind steadily blows,
though in no resolved direction.

Its meandering somehow confirms me,
soothes me the way the night will relieve

this day from its obligations.
As anticipated, the grape leaves

are just beginning to collect rain now,
and when the weight is too much, they

simply turn their wrists, then right themselves
to begin again. I sense no suffering in these

unfinished dreams. Those of the grape leaves,
the uncertain wind, the pine tree locked in praise

every day; not even this room which I've seen
make a prisoner of light, can impose sorrow

upon me while I sit waiting on the
gathering clouds, growing heavy

with a darkness they will offer completely.

To a Distant Friend

The robins continue to search the lawn for
gold Spanish coins, though from childhood

I remember it wasn't coins they buried,
but small ocean-smoothed shards of

green glass. One robin in particular hops
no more than three hops before cocking its head

for a closer inspection, and twitching its tail—
its soft under-feathers being pushed into a grey

crease in the late summer breeze. The rotting willow,
which somehow awakens every spring, has

awakened again. Its leaves are already turning
yellow at the tips, and are sharply pointed

like thousands of arrows aiming for the
earth's core, I think to remind us the earth

is not indifferent. It could let us go at any time,
but continues along its orbit, recalling an ancient

duty to embrace this outrageous paradox
of living things. When a raven clicks its beak

from the massive fir tree just east of the house,
the robins all retreat to the knot of snowberry

shrubs, salal and the single oak tree behind
the old willow. I haven't yet uncovered

the raven's conspiracy with the robins, but I will.
Cars and people pass, sending muffled noises through

to where I sit as I recall the things you adored
about this place—the things that remain unaltered

by the years that have passed since you left.

Sick Christmas

Crows hunched
in the sleeping trees,
pigeons crowding each other
along the line, words
rising from such things
as the snow rotting
under the oaks,
as the sun travelling
unspeakable miles
to lie finally upon the rotting snow.

A child once said:

TÁN, STIWIEⱠ TᖶE NE S'HELI EȾ NEȻE

Mother, my life is a prayer for you.

He knew she was dying,
the child. The mother knew
that her child could see her dying,
that she could no longer hide
her dying from him.

The crows still hunched, wet
and cold and fading into night.
The pigeons going, as one body,
away then back again to the line,
the sun flickering dully as the line
rocks with no birds on it,

and the words?
With the dying we risk them.
They are beyond consequences.

When I Have Learned Too Many Words
for Bill

I was watching the ravens:
one sick and three others
helping it to die. It was like
being in a room full of strangers
and having no place to sit down,
a moment when words must labour
to belong, no place to stand
up and say "This is wrong."

The sick one, no longer
attempting to walk away, was
hunched over and under its sparse
feathers its grey skin was turning
purple and red. One more raven

seemed to be the leader and did
not join in the others' offering
to Death, but followed beside as
an older man hearing a younger man's troubles
walks with his hands behind his back.

The coffee shop where we'd planned to meet
was full, and crowds sometimes make me ill
at ease. I can't stand people thinking of
other things, *their* things.

How can I explain
what relief came:
a hand-up offered to someone
who had been treading
water, drowning at the
bottom of a well?
Or maybe my mother's arms
ready to receive me when
I was young enough
and small enough
to feel lost forever
in a crowd?

Once we spotted each other,
I noticed for the first time
the peace you'd made with
growing old. You waved me over.
You patted the empty seat beside you.

The Gift of the Day
for Tanya Gillman

We've come to the praying place,
the honest place. The camas break
into daylight first, bright violet flowers
shining from history in through her eyes.
Just weeks earlier she gathered the story
of these camas, of the old Saanich man
who stole them from his lost island
and planted them here
to feed his unborn grandchildren.
See him in his canoe
paddling atop the day's first light?

The first gift of this day: her smile
breaking slowly as she turns. That smile
again and again in the imagination
before and after it finally occurred,
broke into the morning of the harvest,
her fist full of broken flowers
her body gripped by realization:
dig into *this* ground: camas,
father, mother, grandfather. . .
soft eyes decayed terribly in the skulls,
but the vision remains.

She can no longer come here without them,
listen, see or love here without them.
Hard bulbs planted in a soft earth,
their flowers would claim the entire planet now—
if she let them, if she wanted them to.

Another gift of this day: real light
finally breaking over the wedge-forest of maples
into the open field. Her smile looked for one
more time, not defined by a false dawn,
but by this new light—this new gift-day.

The Old People say: *Remain asleep
and in bed when the day is breaking
and you will forget the day is a gift.*

Do you see? She still has those broken flowers
in her hand
and she always will.

Justice in Family

Aimed in the same direction—
this is how the family begins
for children.

Now, the four brothers sit together
by the fire. At least as weary
as the adults they could not
so long ago even imagine being
the likeness of, they have decided
the will is not enough and so it is
now burning in a sharply pointed fire.

This fire etches the night it is under
into the talons and tail of a dark bird,
which lifts from the brothers
something that all families must
find a way around or through.

Four boys at the same fire would
fall into the flames forever, like
arms they had no choice but to go to.

But the four brothers, thankfully,
are men and have allowed a time
for shameless tears. Each cries
in his particular way, for his
own reason, yet, each knows
he owes at least his tears.

What We Call Life
for Jacob

1. *HELI*

My nephew calls the dog. The dog's name
is HELI, which means *lively* and *alive*
in the same breath. When my nephew calls
the dog he means the dog and nothing else,
as at six years old naming and possessing
are barely separate. It is a delicate matter,
now more than ever: words such as these
were once regarded as path-markers pointed
toward the more complex world. My nephew
doesn't speak this language, our language,
and may never speak it, yet the countryside
he is so comfortably encrusted in screams
long and steady all around him every day.
There, a tree with no name: it is silent
because it doesn't come from here. But beside it
the *water drinker* with its *twisted heart*
is madly red and ragged while it sheds the year's
outer layer. Its skin rolls off in brittle curls,
ends of the vowel of a scream. Every Saanich
child will eventually confess to having tried smoking
the red and yellow 'cigarettes' scattered at the *feet*
of the tree. *The water drinker's twisted heart?*
A great man once put his hand down in the crown
of a sapling and by some uncommon ability
twisted its heart, proclaiming from then on all
water drinkers would be born with the same affliction.
And that kind of power, it is still in us? Even now?

2. S'HELI

Not forgetting it is a word rooted in *alive*
and *lively* in one breath, S'HELI means *life*.
It could as easily be translated as *awareness*.
For now this means myself and my eldest brother
living day-to-day in the house
that was once our parents'. In the hallways
of this very house, when I was eighteen,
I felt the presence of ancient beings all around me,
breathing shallow breaths. I understand now
their crease is in the pages of my unwritten poems
and along the centre of my secret aches, the kind
reserved for journal entries. At that moment
of quiet and calm, the older people say you are
feeling your S'HELI. When my nephew was only
thirteen days old, I wrote a poem for him.
In my daydreams he was already old enough
to grasp the first layers of the story of Saanich:
how an elder pointed down after the flood,
heart tender from suffering, eyes sharp from tenderness
and said, NI—*Look,* NI QENNET TTE W̱,SÁNEĆ—*Look
what's emerging.* What poetry was to me in those days:
me reading the poem to my mother as we sat
in the hallways of the house. In her tears at the end
of that poem I recall seeing more clearly than could have
been spoken, her urging me to carry on, to keep going.

3. *SOX,HELI*

Finally there is this word implying our true
nature, our *personal belief*; and the story of
my mother's love for salal berries. She believed
their power was so sacred it could *only* be belittled
by words, so we went out at daybreak so she could
show me how to harvest and prepare them properly.
Then, by the dream-light of false dawn, she taught me
the pathway of words: morning, harvest, goodness, salal. . .
Having never attempted a salal berry pie, we waited
nervously at tea and cribbage for the pie to cool.
The pie wasn't that good. But we ate it knowing
the plants had given their *gift*, and it was healthy
to preserve this belief about a harvest and keep it
alive in the family. Feeling silly enough to allow
the edges of our mouths to become purple all around,
she taught me the proper uses of the harvest words.
Talking with her mouth full, life for
the moment entirely in jest, it occurred to me
too many have already come and gone
without ever knowing how sweet life can be.

Giving and Giving

Sometimes I find her
lying in bed upon the heart-
shaped leaf large enough to
enfold her. She's not weeping;
she is too frightened for tears.
Right now she is waiting,
as we have learned to wait,
for the second swell of tears
that follows the first.

This would be the myth
again, of the first healer
who by feigning infancy
called for himself a good
mother to be raised by.

But we are growing *ourselves* up now.

She is staring out from
infancy's hindrance, and
its gift. She is lying upon
the leaf with her head at
the pointed end. Cracks
in the leaf, parallel to her
body, tell me she has had it
pulled around her; it is
a kind of waiting for tears.

I have arrived here with her
before. And we will return here again.
In her eyes an eased look grows,
because she knows it is me and
that I would not fault her for
her need to speak in this wordless,
armless language: the one owned
by the return to infancy, lying
upon a heart-shaped leaf.

And what's more,
sometimes it is me who is
found lying upon the leaf,
feigning infancy to be held
in less ambiguous arms
inside the name
of less ambiguous times.

Taking the Names Down from the Hill

What is Saanich to me now?
Merely the sheer promise
of Matthew before his death,

merely my father's suffering fight
against *his own* death,

merely the painful pierce of doubt
through to my mother
before her death,

and forever the wisdom
we need and will continue to need
rotting out in hollows
in Uncle Gabriel's bones,
under pounds of earth.

It pleases me to be angry,
to be angry and to speak and to write it.
I'm glad, finally,
to have shrunk down Saanich
—what I imagined to be Saanich—
and put it away.

What I imagined was my only home
lost forever under tons of concrete
and vulgar electric houses humming
the sickness into us.

What I imagined to be the only rightness
worth striving for or dying for and making
their deaths right.

Sorrow was pathetic and laden
with a silence so vast that
the drummer could not wake us.

The people went into the hills.
They went there together as one body
knowing who they were
to bring the names home.

Where are the ancestors
we keep calling ourselves?

And while the roadways were being imposed,
the crowns were cast aside and tangled
and will never be brought home
and never properly given.

However, sorrow has had its time.
The mourning must break

at last. I will tell you
what they really left us.
They left us
magic in everything,

the *beautiful way*
in everything. But what
we truly own has never left us:

magic in word,
magic in thought,
magic in song,
magic in touch,

and, yes, magic in the breath
that joins them.

I went to the hills alone
with what I'd shrunk Saanich to
in a few measly pores of the lifeline
of the palm of my hand.

From there,
where it was unceremoniously cradled,
I blew it out over the cobwebbed underbrush
four paces off the footpath
and felt that my work was done
without even singing a song.

On the way back down I stopped
and touched the road but twenty paces
from someone's house,
someone I've never even met
and breathed out *Saanich,*
this is Saanich.

I began to dance. I danced
at least as foolishly as a Scotsman
gone Indian, naked in the woods!
(Or an Irishman for that matter.)

I named and renamed everything
that I spied with my little eye:
Saanich. And my dance?

When I figured I had it down,
that I had it just right, I knew
it was time, as it is for us all.

So by the gift of this
old unapologetic magic
I called it the *Dance of Forever,*

our newest tradition.

Anecdote for this Father and Son

Grade five I hung onto every word,
waiting for the one that would set me free.
When I told my father I wanted to drop out
and he asked why, I said:
School is brainwashing.

Recognizing the resurrection of
his very words he thought forgotten,
he had to be clever,
because cleverness is really the child's
game to delight in.

Well, says the father,
*if you're not gonna get an education,
you're gonna have to learn hard labour.*

Still, in his agonizing studies through night,
the son beholds the vision of the stone
he'd marked with an X—
found for a third time in the field
where he'd been labouring—
and the greater vision of his father
going out again at daybreak with pails of
stones to put in the October fields
where, for the first time, they belonged.